INTRODUCTION TO

THE
TRUE
NATURE
OF
GOD

THE IMPORTANCE AND BENEFITS OF
UNDERSTANDING GOD'S CHARACTER

Andrew Wommack

Published in partnership between Andrew Wommack Ministries and Harrison House Publishers

Woodland Park, CO 80862 - Shippensburg, PA 17257

ISBN 13 TP: 978-1-6675-0243-4

For Worldwide Distribution, Printed in the USA

1 2 3 4 5 6 / 25 24 23 22

Contents

Introduction

Did you know that if a person really knew God and understood Him as the wonderful Father He is, it would not be hard to believe Him and His Word? It would not be hard to receive from Him. I personally believe that faith is a direct result of knowing God better. But if you don't know Him very well, Satan can say all kinds of false things to discredit Him that you will just accept.

You know, if people told me that my wife, Jamie, had been unfaithful to me while I was traveling in ministry, they would just be barking up the wrong tree. Why? Because I know her! It is possible to come into relationship with others to the point that you know what they would be like and what they would do in any set of circumstances. Can you see that? Your relationship with God is no different. He wants you to be assured that you can trust Him to act on your behalf no matter what the situation is.

One of the reasons many Christians find it so hard to believe God is because they have misunderstood Him. They don't know His true nature. They haven't developed personal relationship with Him. They may know some things *about* God, but if they knew Him intimately, it would take the struggle out of the Christian life.

The Word of God is so simple you have to have somebody help you misunderstand it. The biggest problem is that people don't really hear. They're thinking about what they had for breakfast, where they're going to eat lunch, or about this or that. So, before I move into this material, I'm sharing with you that some of my points may seem radical or somewhat dramatic. But it's the truth. I really want you to understand the nature of God like you never have. If you will receive what I'm saying, no one will ever be able to talk you out of God's goodness toward you. I'm believing that as you read, your life will be changed forever!

A Better Understanding

The only way we can truly know anything about God is through the Bible. Everybody on the earth has an opinion about what God is like and what He will do. He's been so misrepresented. But it's the Word that is going to tell us who He is for sure. Now, some people do read and study God's Word; however, even among them, a lot of passages in the Bible appear to give a "schizophrenic" revelation of God. In one scripture, God commands death by stoning for picking up sticks on the Sabbath day (Num. 15:32–35), and then in another, He forgives and does not condemn a woman caught in the very act of adultery (John 8:3–11). Examples like these have polarized and confused believers for years. Some will say, "Well, you just can't know what God's really like." But that isn't true. We just need a better understanding of His Word.

The Old Testament Is Incomplete

One of the first things you must understand is that the Word of God does not contradict itself. There is a perfect harmony to it all. Much of what is in this booklet purposes to harmonize the Old and New Testaments to reach a better, more complete understanding of the nature of God.

In the Old Testament, we see a picture of God that is incomplete. Therefore, people who create their understanding of the nature of God based only on the Old Testament don't end up with a fully accurate picture. Unless we understand the Old Testament in light of the New, we are going to struggle to understand who it is we are really dealing with.

As I have said before and will say many times throughout this booklet, we have to come to a place where we really know God and have intimate relationship with Him. That is what He has always wanted for us. But most of us have accepted Old Testament ideas about Him that have blocked us from that. Many of us are afraid to draw near because we've been taught that

We have to come
to a place where we
really know God
and have intimate
relationship
with Him.

He is going to "hit" us with something. That is not even close to what the Word really teaches.

Old Testament Judgment

Let's look at an example of how things were done in the Old Testament. Elijah was one of the few prophets of the Lord. Wicked kings had been killing them because they stood for righteousness and worship of the true God (1 Kgs. 18:13). King Ahaziah was one of these kings. He'd been seeking after pagan gods. When he got sick, instead of inquiring of God for his healing, he sent messengers to Baalzebub, the god of Ekron.

According to 2 Kings 1:3–8, Ahaziah's messengers were on their way to inquire of Baalzebub. Read what happened next:

> But the angel of the LORD said to Elijah the Tishbite, Arise, go up to meet the messengers of the king of Samaria, and say unto them, Is it not because there is not a God in Israel, that ye go to enquire of Baalzebub the god of Ekron? Now therefore thus saith the LORD, Thou shalt not come down from that bed on which thou art gone

up, but shalt surely die. And Elijah departed. And when the messengers turned back unto him, he said unto them, Why are ye now turned back? And they said unto him, There came a man up to meet us, and said unto us, Go, turn again unto the king that sent you, and say unto him, Thus saith the LORD, Is it not because there is not a God in Israel, that thou sendest to enquire of Baalzebub the god of Ekron? therefore thou shalt not come down from that bed on which thou art gone up, but shalt surely die. And he said unto them, What manner of man was he which came up to meet you, and told you these words? And they answered him, He was an hairy man, and girt with a girdle of leather about his loins. And he said, It is Elijah the Tishbite.

The king knew it was Elijah and was seized with fear, so he sent his armies out to capture him.

Then the king sent unto him a captain of fifty with his fifty. And he went up to him: and, behold, he sat on the top of an hill. And he spake unto him, Thou man of God, the king hath said, Come down. And Elijah answered and said to the captain of fifty, If I be a man of God, then let fire come down from heaven, and consume thee and thy fifty. And there came down fire from heaven, and consumed him and his fifty.

2 Kings 1:9–10

That's pretty strong, isn't it? You just didn't mess with Elijah!

Again also he sent unto him another captain of fifty with his fifty. And he answered and said unto him, O man of God, thus hath the king said, Come down quickly. And Elijah answered and said unto them, If I be a man of God, let fire come down from heaven, and consume thee and thy fifty. And the fire of God came down from heaven, and consumed him and his fifty.

2 Kings 1:11–12

That's 102 men! Elijah had access to the power of God to such a degree that he could consume people. But did you know that's not the only way Elijah could have handled the problem? This is an Old Testament example of the power, the anointing, and the wrath of God in defense of one of His prophets.

New Testament Grace

L et's compare this story of Elijah with a story in
Luke:

*And it came to pass, when the time was come that
he should be received up, he stedfastly set his face
to go to Jerusalem, And sent messengers before his
face: and they went, and entered into a village of
the Samaritans, to make ready for him. And they
did not receive him, because his face was as though
he would go to Jerusalem.*

Luke 9:51–53

There was tremendous hatred involving religious
and racial prejudices between the Jews and the Samaritans. The Jews would have no dealings with them at
all (John 4:9). But Jesus loved them and ministered to
them. They had accepted Him as the Messiah. By the
time of Luke 9, Jesus was coming through their town
again, and they rejected Him because He was going to
those "hypocrites" down in Jerusalem. To reject Jesus
under these circumstances was pretty serious, and

two of His disciples had a knee-jerk, Old Testament reaction:

And when his disciples James and John saw this, they said, Lord, wilt thou that we command fire to come down from heaven, and consume them, even as Elias did?

Luke 9:54

Certainly, James and John were as justified in wanting to kill the Samaritans for their rejection of Jesus as Elijah was in calling fire down to kill the soldiers who had rejected the God of Israel, right? Yet look how Jesus responded to His disciples:

But he turned, and rebuked them, and said, Ye know not what manner of spirit ye are of. For the Son of man is not come to destroy men's lives, but to save them.

Luke 9:55–56

Jesus rebuked James and John for trying to do what was done under the Old Testament! Does that mean Elijah was sinning in 2 Kings 1? No, because at that time, God was dealing with man differently, in the only way He could at the time.

Harmonizing Old and New Testaments

When people understand God with an Old Testament mindset, they generally picture Him as a God of wrath, judgment, and punishment. That is *a* truth about God, and those who don't accept the love and forgiveness of the Lord Jesus Christ will one day experience a terrible day of God's judgment. But wrath and judgment are not the essential nature of God.

God's nature is not judgment. You can't find that in the Word of God. He does judge, and He is just and holy to do so. But Scripture reveals to us in 1 John 4:8 that *"God is love."* He doesn't just *have* love or *operate* in love; God *is* love. That is His real nature! The Old Testament cannot give you this revelation of God by itself. You need to harmonize the Old Testament with the New Testament to understand the fullness of God.

In the beginning was the Word, and the Word was with God, and the Word was God . . . . And the Word was made flesh, and dwelt among us, (and

Wrath and judgment are not the essential nature of God.

we beheld his glory, the glory as of the only begotten of the Father,) full of grace and truth.

John 1:1, 14

Jesus saith unto him, Have I been so long time with you, and yet hast thou not known me, Philip? he that hath seen me hath seen the Father; and how sayest thou then, Shew us the Father?

John 14:9

Jesus is the walking, living Word. When we see Him, we see the Father. So, the problem many Christians are facing is that they are seeing God through the Old Testament instead of through Jesus! They misunderstand and are confused about who God really is and the relationship He wants with them because they are seeing Him through the Old Testament, where He had to deal with mankind and sin in a different manner. In the following chapters, we are going to look at many scriptures that tell us that. But to briefly help make this point here, look at this passage from Hebrews:

God, who at sundry times and in divers manners spake in time past unto the fathers by the prophets, Hath in these last days spoken unto us by his Son,

You need to harmonize the Old Testament with the New Testament to understand the fullness of God.

whom he hath appointed heir of all things, by whom also he made the worlds; Who being the brightness of his glory, and the express image of his person, and upholding all things by the word of his power, when he had by himself purged our sins, sat down on the right hand of the Majesty on high; Being made so much better than the angels, as he hath by inheritance obtained a more excellent name than they.

Hebrews 1:1–4

In verse 3, it says Jesus is the brightness of God's glory and the express image of His person. In other words, Jesus is an exact representation of God—His true nature revealed! Therefore, when we read, for example, that Jesus laid down His life because of His great love for us (John 3:16; 1 John 3:16; 4:10), we can be sure that this is a clear picture of what God is like.

Most of us don't really recognize or understand the depth of the love, mercy, and compassion that God offers us through Jesus Christ. When we mistakenly misunderstand the Word, it keeps us at arm's length from Him. We must harmonize the Old and New Testaments in order to clearly see: God is not schizophrenic!

God's Grace
in the Old Testament

Now, you can see God's love and grace in the Old Testament, which reveals that His nature is consistent throughout the entire Bible. By the time of Genesis 6, sin was pervasive on the face of the earth. Read what it says in verse 6:

> *And it repented the LORD that he had made man on the earth, and it grieved him at his heart.*

Genesis 6:6

God is long-suffering, and for Him to grieve that He even made mankind, people must have trespassed against Him greatly. Years after He judged them through the Flood, He finally gave Moses the Old Testament Law. By stating emphatically what was right and what was wrong and by giving mankind His perfect standard, God was saying, "Here is proof that your sin is unacceptable." But did you know that the giving of the Law was never His desire? If it had been, He would have communicated it to Adam and Eve in the Garden, right after they sinned.

The primary reason God waited 2,500 years before giving the Law to Moses is because it is the goodness of God that leads man to repentance (Rom 2:4). Again, this goes back to His true nature. God never wanted man to try to obey His perfect standard or face wrath; He wanted them to love Him because of His goodness and mercy. However, there is another reason God did not give Adam and Eve the Law: God did not want Adam and Eve to know the terribleness and depths of their sin.

Can you imagine what it would have been like for them if they would have understood what their sin was really going to do to the human race? Can you imagine what it would have been like if they had been given a glimpse of the billions of people who would go to hell throughout all eternity because of what they had done? Can you imagine if they had had a graphic picture of all the suffering, tragedy, wars, and atrocities that their sin was going to cause? What would that have done to them? They would not have been able to tolerate that realization. I don't think they would have been able to live with it.

God wanted to operate in love and mercy toward Adam and Eve, so He did not impute sin to them by giving them the Law (Rom. 5:13). If they and their

God never wanted man to try to obey His perfect standard or face wrath.

descendants had understood God's view of sin, hopelessness would have set in on the human race to such a degree that they wouldn't have been able to believe He offered them mercy or forgiveness. They would not have been able to expect help from Him and would have turned themselves over to Satan instead.

By showing man mercy, love, and forgiveness, God was drawing them to Himself, that they might accept His promise of redemption through the coming Messiah and be saved. However, man began to go further away from Him, yielding themselves more and more to Satan. Through sin, Satan was literally destroying the human race! So, God handed down the Law to Moses. Again, this was not His first choice, but it was the only choice mankind gave Him.

The Purpose for the Old Testament Law

We have discussed how the Old Testament is not an exact representation of God, but it goes much deeper than that. The Old Covenant was an inferior covenant to the New Covenant. The whole book of Hebrews addresses this concept in detail, but here are a few scriptures to illustrate my point.

> *But now hath he obtained a more excellent ministry, by how much also he is the mediator of a better covenant, which was established upon better promises. For if that first covenant had been faultless, then should no place have been sought for the second.*
>
> Hebrews 8:6–7

> *In that he saith, A new covenant, he hath made the first old. Now that which decayeth and waxeth old is ready to vanish away.*
>
> Hebrews 8:13

By so much was Jesus made a surety of a better testament.

Hebrews 7:22

The Old Covenant couldn't make anything perfect, so God had to bring in something better. This was the New Covenant, which was sealed by the shed blood of Jesus Christ. The New Covenant brought greater glory to God than the Old Covenant.

But if the ministration of death, written and engraven in stones, was glorious, so that the children of Israel could not stedfastly behold the face of Moses for the glory of his countenance; which glory was to be done away: How shall not the ministration of the spirit be rather glorious? For if the ministration of condemnation be glory, much more doth the ministration of righteousness exceed in glory. For even that which was made glorious had no glory in this respect, by reason of the glory that excelleth. For if that which is done away was glorious, much more that which remaineth is glorious.

2 Corinthians 3:7–11

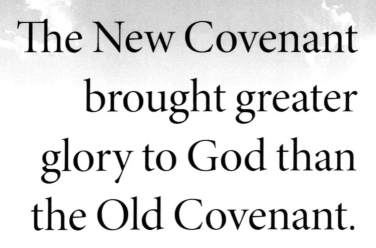

The New Covenant brought greater glory to God than the Old Covenant.

This passage of Scripture also says that the Old Testament administers death and condemnation!

O death, where is thy sting? O grave, where is thy victory? The sting of death is sin; and the strength of sin is the law.

1 Corinthians 15:55–56

Paul is saying that the Old Testament Law gave strength to sin! The Old Testament Law strengthened our enemy: sin. It didn't strengthen us. I know this may be challenging your theology. In fact, this may just make everything tilt on the inside of you. But you may need to come to grips with some truths to harmonize the Old Testament Law with New Testament grace, love, and forgiveness.

Now we know that what things soever the law saith, it saith to them who are under the law: that every mouth may be stopped, and all the world may become guilty before God.

Romans 3:19

Have you ever felt guilty? Do you know where that came from? You got that through the Law—through the Old Testament administration. The Law makes you feel guilty. It condemns you, according to this verse and 2 Corinthians 3:9—

For if the ministration of condemnation be glory, much more doth the ministration of righteousness exceed in glory.

Condemnation is not to be confused with the conviction of the Holy Spirit, however. Conviction draws you to God and leads you into relationship with Him. But condemnation drives you *away* from intimacy with God and makes you feel helpless to do anything about your sin. You'll feel trapped—saved but stuck!

Most of us as believers would agree that Satan is the author of condemnation, but one of the biggest things he uses to minister condemnation to us is the Old Testament Law. We frequently rebuke the condemnation of the devil, but sometimes condemnation comes from thoughts established in us through religion. We need to cleanse ourselves from thoughts that have Old Testament scriptures attached to them.

Therefore by the deeds of the law there shall no flesh be justified in his sight: for by the law is the knowledge of sin.

Romans 3:20

The Bible says that the purpose of the Law is to give us the knowledge of sin, not the knowledge of Jesus. It drew our attention to ourselves and our unworthiness.

You might be thinking, *Who cares about the Old Covenant? I don't offer blood sacrifices. I don't kill goats and sheep. I'm not under the Old Covenant.* You may not be doing any of these things, but I promise you, your theology, thinking, and attitudes are probably influenced by the Old Covenant to some degree or another. You may be offering works of self-sacrifice and self-punishment to atone for your sin and guilt. It's like you've changed cars but are headed down the same road to the same destination.

The religious attitude of the Law will keep you focused on your sin and, therefore, from walking in intimacy with God. You'll only see His wrath, judgment, and punishment and will wind up with such a sense of unworthiness and guilt; you will run *from* God instead of *to* Him—the only one who can actually free you from sin!

The religious attitude of the Law will keep you focused on your sin.

God's Grace
for the Believer

Let no man therefore judge you in meat, or in drink, or in respect of an holyday, or of the new moon, or of the sabbath days: Which are a shadow of things to come; but the body is of Christ.

Colossians 2:16–17

The Old Testament was just a shadow of things that were to come. According to this passage of Scripture, it was not the exact image of things the way God wanted them to be. The way He dealt with people under the Old Covenant was not His preference. Somebody may say, "But doesn't God do whatever He wants to do?"

I could spend a lot of time on this, but to put it in a nutshell, not everything that happens is what God wants to happen. This is because He gave mankind free will. God committed a tremendous amount of authority to us when He gave Adam dominion over the earth (Gen. 1:26, 28), and man really messed up His original plan.

People who believe nothing happens except what God ordains to happen get violently upset when I start preaching this! But I can't understand why they get so upset. If nobody could do anything except what God ordained, I couldn't be teaching this unless God ordained me to teach it. So, the people who believe God causes everything to happen contradict themselves by telling me it is not God's will for me to teach this!

The truth is that not every word said and not everything done is totally orchestrated by God. Because of that, God was not able to manifest His perfect will under the Old Covenant as we see through Jesus. The Old Covenant was only a temporary way of dealing with mankind, and it was instituted only until Jesus came. It is sad to say, but most Christians today make no clear distinction between the Old Covenant way God dealt with mankind and the New Covenant way.

When the Old Testament Law was given, people were deceived about sin (Rom. 7:11). Enforcing the Law showed mankind a part of the nature of God—that He was holy, and no unholy thing could stand in His presence—but Jesus provided the entire and complete picture.

For the law was given by Moses, but grace and truth came by Jesus Christ.

John 1:17

Justified by Faith, Not Performance

When people realize their sinful condition, whether by the Law or the knowledge of God's goodness, they start looking to Jesus alone for their salvation. But then, after they are born again, somehow they slip into thinking that God's going to move in their lives in proportion to their personal holiness. Nothing could be further from the truth!

Where did performance-based teaching come from? Believe it or not, it came out of God's Word. It was a misunderstanding of what God was doing in the Old Testament Law. In Deuteronomy 28:1–2, all the blessings of God appear to be conditional on the word "if":

And it shall come to pass, if thou shalt hearken diligently unto the voice of the LORD thy God, to observe and to do all his commandments which I command thee this day, that the LORD thy God will set thee on high above all nations of the earth: And all these blessings shall come on thee, and overtake

thee, if thou shalt hearken unto the voice of the
LORD thy God.

Verse 1 says that we have to do all of God's commandments, not just some of them. If we would just stop and think a moment, we would realize that we have never kept all the commandments of God.

Therefore to him that knoweth to do good, and
doeth it not, to him it is sin.

James 4:17

Sin is more than just doing what we know is wrong; it also is not doing what we know is right. If we look at sin from God's standpoint, none of us have measured up but Jesus. None of us have become sinless in our flesh, in our actions, and in our performance. We're all still missing the mark. Therefore, we will only have peace with God if we are justified by faith in the finished work of Jesus Christ and not our works (Rom. 5:1).

Then, in Romans 5:8, Paul wrote, *"But God commendeth his love toward us, in that, while we were yet sinners, Christ died for us."* What he was saying is that God did not give His love to us *based on our performance.* When we were still sinners, even haters of God and still going

We will only have peace with God if we are justified by faith in the finished work of Jesus Christ.

our own way, God gave us His most precious gift: the Lord Jesus Christ. We didn't deserve it, and our performance hadn't earned it. Right in the midst of our sin, God commended His love toward us. Hallelujah!

Walking in More Grace

In Romans 5:9, Paul concluded with his main point:

Much more then, being now justified by his blood, we shall be saved from wrath through him.

In other words, if we can accept the fact that God showed His love toward us when Jesus died for us while we were sinners—*much more* now that we are justified by His blood—we shall be saved from God's wrath.

Do you follow the point Paul was making? He was saying that if we could accept the love, mercy, and forgiveness of God while we were sinners, we should be able to accept the love, mercy, and forgiveness of God much more now that we're His children! As Christians, we ought to be walking even more freely in the grace of God than we were when we came to Him for salvation.

Look at this verse:

As ye have therefore received Christ Jesus the Lord, so walk ye in him: Rooted and built up in him.

Colossians 2:6–7a

The principle we applied to receive salvation from the Lord should be the same principle by which we walk with the Lord. If our works were not the basis for receiving salvation from God, why should our works be a factor in receiving anything else from God? This Bible verse says we should keep going with God on the same basis as we started!

When people come to the altar for salvation, they know it is not in direct proportion to their performance. Yet when it comes to healing, prosperity, deliverance, answers to prayer, and so forth, many of them believe they will receive from God according to their performance.

The Bible says that sin is sin. James 2:10 says, *"For whosoever shall keep the whole law, and yet offend in one point, he is guilty of all."* If you have led a good life and yet you miss it in one part, you don't deserve anything from God! That is what this scripture is communicating.

That was the purpose of the Old Testament Law. It showed us our sin, which condemned so we would quit trying to please the Lord by our performance and accept relationship with Him by faith in His sacrifice, Jesus.

We ought to be walking even more freely in the grace of God than we were when we came to Him for salvation.

We need to stop approaching God on the basis of what we have done. We need to come to God for every need the way we came to Him for salvation: through the finished work of Jesus Christ!

How to Be Blessed by God

Most Christians can accept that they are redeemed from the curse of the Law listed in Deuteronomy 28:15–68. The Scripture says,

Christ hath redeemed us from the curse of the law, being made a curse for us: for it is written, Cursed is every one that hangeth on a tree.

Galatians 3:13

However, those same Christians are generally not bold enough to demand the blessings listed in Deuteronomy 28:1–14. Why? Because they know in their hearts that they haven't fulfilled Deuteronomy 28:1–2, which says that all the blessings are conditional, based upon obeying all the commandments.

And it shall come to pass, if thou shalt hearken diligently unto the voice of the LORD thy God, to observe and to do all his commandments which I command thee this day, that the LORD thy God will set thee on high above all nations of the earth: And

all these blessing shall come on thee, and overtake thee, if thou shalt hearken unto the voice of the LORD thy God.

Deuteronomy 28:1–2

I do believe there are benefits to obeying God's commands. I can tell you, the reason I live a holy life is because I don't want Satan having inroads into my life. I can't afford the "luxury" of him putting problems on me. I try to live holy as a defense against the devil and as a testimony to other people. As often as you can be obedient to God, you will shut the door on Satan. If you keep 50 percent of God's commandments, you will shut the door to Satan 50 percent of the time. The less place you give to him, the better off you will be. But if you don't live a holy life, God will love you just the same. It was never meant to be a basis for relationship with Him or to get Him to bless you. That was accomplished through what Jesus did for you, not what you do for Jesus.

When we sin and give place to the devil, we just need to repent, restore our intimacy with God, and boot the devil out! The Scripture says,

As often as you can be obedient to God, you will shut the door on Satan.

Submit yourselves therefore to God. Resist the devil, and he will flee from you.

James 4:7

The correct way New Testament saints should read Deuteronomy 28:1–2 is to say that the blessings of God are coming to pass in our lives since *Jesus* kept all of the commandments of God and hearkened diligently to them. According to Romans 8:4, Jesus—who was perfect—gave Himself as a sacrifice so that *"the righteousness of the law might be fulfilled in us."*

Because of Jesus, all of *His* righteousness has been committed to us so that the righteousness of the Law is fulfilled in *us.* According to 2 Corinthians 5:21, *"He hath made him to be sin for us, who knew no sin; that we might be made the righteousness of God in him."* We should declare that we are now the righteousness of God; therefore, all these commandments are fulfilled, and the blessings are coming upon us and overtaking us *through what Jesus did!*

The Knowledge
of Him

Because we haven't really understood the nature and the character of God, we haven't understood how He deals with us and why He answers prayer. Therefore, we haven't been allowing Him to truly manifest Himself in our lives by meeting our needs.

His divine power hath given unto us all things that pertain unto life and godliness, through the knowledge of him that hath called us to glory and virtue.

2 Peter 1:3

God said, *"all things that pertain unto life and godliness."* Did you know that includes healing, joy, deliverance, prosperity, and anything you can think of that comes as a result of our redemption? These all come through *"the knowledge of Him."* If you have wrong knowledge about God, you are not going to receive the *"all things!"*

You'll be looking for judgment, punishment, and for Him to withhold what you are asking for in prayer. You'll get what you expect or believe. Jesus affirmed this in many places, including Matthew 9:29: *"According to your faith be it unto you."* But when you understand the true nature of God, you will realize that all of His fullness is yours (John 1:16).

The truth is, we can live in a realm where we are so intimate with God that things will work for us. And I believe that's the way of life God is drawing His people into—why we are talking about knowing God. If we really focus on knowing Him, everything else will work out of that. But when the Word becomes technical details and formulas concerning the mechanics of Christianity, we lose our focus. We are doing things in our own strength and not His. We are trying to impress Him with works instead of being impressed by His works and who He is.

As I've said at the beginning of this booklet, if you develop your personal relationship with God to the point that you understand how much God loves you, it will not be hard to believe He is going to supply your every need.

We can live in a realm where we are so intimate with God that things will work for us.

If you are struggling to receive from God, you just need to know Him better. When you really know Him, you will be totally convinced of His love and that He'll meet your needs. You won't have any more fear.

I have found the place of peace in the Lord where, if blow it, I know it doesn't break my fellowship with Him. I know He still loves me and will still use me to minister to others. So, if someone needs prayer, I don't look at whether I've lived good or bad that day. I know I can shoot my best shot for them and get them healed through who Jesus is and not through who Andrew Wommack is. Praise God!

When you really know Him, you will be totally convinced of His love and that He'll meet your needs.

God's New Wine

We've been learning about the nature and the character of God and the reason for understanding His true nature. We have seen how God has dealt with mankind from the time of Adam to the present. We've also seen that the Old Testament complements the New Testament and points toward the New Covenant. The Old Testament prepared the way for the New Testament. But if we try to live under the New Covenant and the Old Covenant at the same time, it's like taking new wine and putting it into old wineskins (Luke 5:37–38): The old wineskins are going to burst, and the wine will run out. It's like trying to sew a new patch on an old piece of clothing (Luke 5:36). When the clothing is washed and dried, the new patch is going to shrink. Since the old fabric doesn't have any shrinkage left, the garment will tear.

Begin depending on and resting in what Jesus has done, instead of what we've done. When we do this, we are putting the new wine in a *new* wineskin!

Conclusion

What I've presented is really very simple, and every Christian deserves to know it. It is sad to say, but I think not more than one of out of a thousand Christians has this accurate concept of the nature of God.

Most of us approached God without recognizing our redemption and what Jesus really did for us. We were in a constant mode of trying to perform. We've been putting faith in what we did instead of putting faith in what Jesus did. And as soon as Satan pointed out something we did wrong, we started condemning ourselves and telling God we now understood why something wasn't working in our lives.

When it comes to healing, prosperity, or deliverance, we tend to look at what we've done and say, "God, we've been doing the best we can—is it enough?" No, it's not enough, and it never will be!

We have been studying the Word, praying in tongues, and doing all kinds of spiritual things we ought to do. But we need to do them to build *ourselves* up and know Him better, not to try to make Him want to bless us or to give Him a better impression of us. We should do these things to stay strong and finish strong in this spiritual race. The reason I confess the Word of God or pray in tongues is not to move God, but to move myself closer to Him. Holiness doesn't change God's attitude toward me, but it changes my attitude toward Him.

Maybe approaching God by your works doesn't describe you. You know God wants to call you into a secret place of close, intimate communion with Him, but you haven't allowed yourself to approach Him, because you don't feel worthy. You may believe you would be like a hypocrite coming before Him, and He would chastise you, scold you, and say, "How dare you think you have the right to enter into My presence, you sorry worm?"

You may not put it in exactly those words, but perhaps that is your concept. You need to know that according to Romans 8:15, you can always come before God and say, "Papa, Father" or "Abba, Father!" You can come boldly before God and have personal, intimate relationship with Him:

> *Let us therefore come boldly unto the throne of grace, that we may obtain mercy, and find grace to help in time of need.*

> Hebrews 4:16

Holiness doesn't change God's attitude toward me, but it changes my attitude toward Him.

It's the throne of *grace*, not the throne of *works* or the throne of perfect performance. You can do that right now and let God begin to love you.

In either case, you may need to humble yourself before God, saying, "Father, I'm sorry. I have done everything in my own effort. I've misunderstood You. I've been trying to perform. I thought You only gave me things I deserved, and I haven't been depending on Jesus. I've been trying to approach You on my own merit."

When you come into the presence of God, thank Him that you are who He says you are. Focus on Him and let Him minister to you. You'll start reflecting holiness more accidentally than you ever have on purpose. Suddenly, instead of it being drudgery to try to separate yourself and spend time with God, it'll be a blessing.

I know God wants to draw you to Himself right now, as you are reading these words. If you can receive what is presented in this booklet, you will grow in your understanding of His true nature. It will set you free to enjoy a fulfilling and satisfying relationship with God.

This is only a brief summary of an entire book I have, titled *The True Nature of God*. I also have CDs and DVDs that go into more than five hours of teaching on this subject. If this booklet has blessed you, the complete series would be an even greater blessing and help establish you in these New Covenant truths. You can go to my website, awmi.net or call our 24/7 Helpline at (719) 635-1111.

Receive Jesus as Your Savior

Choosing to receive Jesus Christ as your Lord and Savior is the most important decision you'll ever make!

God's Word promises, *"That if thou shalt confess with thy mouth the Lord Jesus, and shalt believe in thine heart that God hath raised him from the dead, thou shalt be saved. For with the heart man believeth unto righteousness; and with the mouth confession is made unto salvation"* (Rom. 10:9–10). *"For whosoever shall call upon the name of the Lord shall be saved"* (Rom. 10:13). By His grace, God has already done everything to provide salvation. Your part is simply to believe and receive.

Pray out loud: "Jesus, I confess that You are my Lord and Savior. I believe in my heart that God raised You from the dead. By faith in Your Word, I receive salvation now. Thank You for saving me."

The very moment you commit your life to Jesus Christ, the truth of His Word instantly comes to pass in your spirit. Now that you're born again, there's a brand-new you!

Receive the Holy Spirit

A s His child, your loving heavenly Father wants to give you the supernatural power you need to live a new life. *"For every one that asketh receiveth; and he that seeketh findeth; and to him that knocketh it shall be opened…how much more shall your heavenly Father give the Holy Spirit to them that ask him?"* (Luke 11:10–13).

All you have to do is ask, believe, and receive!

Pray this: "Father, I recognize my need for Your power to live a new life. Please fill me with Your Holy Spirit. By faith, I receive it right now. Thank You for baptizing me. Holy Spirit, You are welcome in my life."

Congratulations! Now you're filled with God's supernatural power.

Some syllables from a language you don't recognize will rise up from your heart to your mouth (1 Cor. 14:14). As you speak them out loud by faith, you're releasing God's power from within and building yourself up in the spirit (1 Cor. 14:4). You can do this whenever and wherever you like.

It doesn't really matter whether you felt anything or not when you prayed to receive the Lord and His Spirit. If you believed in your heart that you received, then God's Word promises you did. *"Therefore I say unto you, What things soever ye desire, when ye pray, believe that ye receive them, and ye shall have them"* (Mark 11:24). God always honors His Word—believe it!

Please contact me and let me know that you've prayed to receive Jesus as your Savior or be filled with the Holy Spirit. I would like to rejoice with you and help you understand more fully what has taken place in your life. I'll send you a free gift that will help you understand and grow in your new relationship with the Lord.

Welcome to your new life!

Call for Prayer

If you need prayer for any reason, you can call our Prayer Line 24 hours a day, seven days a week at 719-635-1111. A trained prayer minister will answer your call and pray with you. Every day, we receive testimonies of healings and other miracles from our Prayer Line, and we are ministering God's nearly-too-good-to-be-true message of the Gospel to more people than ever. So I encourage you to call today!

About the Author

ANDREW WOMMACK'S life was forever changed the moment he encountered the supernatural love of God on March 23, 1968. As a renowned Bible teacher and author, Andrew has made it his mission to change the way the world sees God.

Andrew's vision is to go as far and deep with the Gospel as possible. His message goes far through the *Gospel Truth* television program, which is available to nearly half the world's population. The message goes deep through discipleship at Charis Bible College, headquartered in Woodland Park, Colorado. Founded in 1994, Charis has campuses across the United States and around the globe.

Andrew also has an extensive library of teaching materials in print, audio, and video—most of which can be accessed for free from his website: awmi.net.